A Letter from God

A Letter from God

We Stand at the Edge of Our Future

Michael A. Reimann

iUniverse, Inc.
Bloomington

A Letter from God
We Stand at the Edge of Our Future

Cover design by Jackie Boston

iUniverse books may be ordered through booksellers or by contacting:

iUniverse
1663 Liberty Drive
Bloomington, IN 47403
www.iuniverse.com
1-800-Authors (1-800-288-4677)

ISBN: 978-1-4620-5115-1 (sc)
ISBN: 978-1-4620-5116-8 (ebk)

Printed in the United States of America

iUniverse rev. date: 09/27/2011

Contents

To our children and grandchildren.

Face the future with optimism and excitement
for its unlimited possibilities.

Preface

The letter that gives this book its title is addressed to the people of Earth, which means everybody. But be warned: what you read in the following pages may not appeal to many of you, particularly if you are devoutly religious.

Faith takes many forms, and the beliefs entrenched in the minds of diverse races over the centuries of human history differ from each other in various ways, many of which conflict with each other. As most readers already know, these conflicts have become physical on many occasions, and racial or religious hate crimes are unfortunately still common throughout the world. Religious doctrines often stand in conflict with modern concepts of human rights. Belief systems passed down through generations do not tend to take easily to change, even in the presence of strong suggestive evidence.

While differences abound, the majority of today's religions have in common the belief in a single deity. What you are about to read will not shake that concept but is hard on the earthly trappings that go with it. There is a harsh reality that must be faced in our future. It is ours to deal with, and while those who think God will provide the answers may well be right, they may be surprised at what those answers turn out to be.

As transcriber of the letter, I have taken the liberty of inserting headings to guide the reader through the rather long discourse. Occasional footnotes refer the interested reader to source materials for further reading.

MAR

Introduction

What, you might ask, qualifies a physicist to write about God? To most beginning students, physics is not particularly inspiring, having a reputation of being difficult, dry, and closely associated with another often dreaded subject, mathematics. After all, physics lacks the exotic smells and exciting special effects of chemistry, the romance of the arts, or the fascination of biology. But wait! Even the dullest subject can shine when brought to life by the right teacher.

Physics is the purest of studies for anyone truly interested in the world and universe we live in. Everything around us, near and far, what we see, touch, and feel, has attributes explained by the laws of physics. Objects are hard or soft, shiny or transparent, liquid or gaseous, because of their atomic and molecular structure. The interaction of molecules with each other that makes chemistry exciting, the fluid dynamics of air that allow heavy jetliners to fly, and the warmth of the sun that gives us life are all what they are because of the operation of the laws of physics. Nature itself is ruled by these laws. The orbits of the planets, the light of the stars, and the composition of the universe follow them absolutely. What better starting point can there be to seek the source of our being than in the study of what shapes our surroundings?

Albert Einstein, Nobel laureate and widely acknowledged as one of the greatest physicists of all time, said this: "I believe in Spinoza's God who reveals himself in the orderly harmony of what exists, not in a God who concerns himself with the fates and actions of human beings." Benedict de Spinoza was a seventeenth-century philosopher who viewed God and Nature as indistinguishable.

The subtitle of this book is *We Stand at the Edge of Our Future.*

Propelled by its biological imperatives, the human race has reached the top of the food chain in Earth's animal kingdom. Dexterity, self-interest, and the power of the brain have combined to make us undisputed masters of our planet. The technology explosion has given us capability far in excess of our natural endowments, and our reservoir of knowledge has passed the ability of any one of us to absorb. With these tremendous advantages, will we be able to control our destiny, or will our human failings overcome us?

As we pass the seven billion mark in the human population of Earth, we are seeing serious signs of impending catastrophe. Starvation and lack of potable water is affecting tens of millions of people in many parts of the world, already being described as humanitarian disaster areas. War, civil unrest, and terrorism headline our daily news. Our collective use of energy is exceeding renewable supplies and causing serious global pollution concerns. We are not living in harmony with our planetary environment, and the rate of our transgression is accelerating. This is not a sustainable course for humanity, and so we are rapidly approaching an edge in the progression of our development. What lies beyond the edge is not an easy path into the future, but the potential of the brains and ingenuity that brought us this far may yet prevail.

The time is upon us to recognize that the course of human history is about to change dramatically, and our part in directing it is critical. In the distant past Moses, a prophet and leader of men revered in three of the world's major religions (Judaism, Christianity, and Islam), brought his followers life-changing rules to live by. The Ten Commandments are still widely quoted to this day, and whether they came directly from the deity or from Moses's ingenuity matters little to their effectiveness. If *A Letter from God* gets you to think about the human condition and the future we may be facing, it has done its work, whether divinely inspired or merely the humble work of this scribe.

Michael A. Reimann
Vancouver, BC
July 2011

The Letter

Dear people of Earth:

This is a letter to you from "God." I have chosen someone to transcribe it because of language issues. You have so many languages and so many names for me that I recognize a difficulty in communicating without imposing a cultural bias. I have chosen English, as it is becoming your most widely spoken language and is as advanced as any in its capability of expressing concepts that touch the edges of your knowledge.

I have disseminated innumerable messages such as this to the ephemeral beings of yours and other universes, of which there are far more than you will ever visualize. You are now at a crucial time in your existence, when your very survival is threatened, and yet you stand to gain from great learning and realization of limitless potential. These communications sometimes help guide their recipients through troubled times to a cleaner future less cluttered with outdated cultural and intellectual baggage of the past.

In your case, religion is a heavy burden you carry, to your great detriment. Disguised in a cloak of benevolence, it harbors fertile seeds of your destruction. Religion is a misguided human failing that has caused your history to be permeated with violence and suffering. It has spawned a host of examples of persecution, unspeakable cruelty, and bloody wars, all based on elaborate belief systems lacking factual foundations. Religions were all created by people, most of whom claimed some sort of communication with one of many forms attributed to me over the ages; all are badly flawed. No doubt their champions were clever, insightful, and able leaders, and many of their rules to live by were appropriate to their times, providing useful behavioral boundaries for the society of their adherents. The founders of Christianity and Islam are prime examples, and indeed overt teachings of these religions offer many positive influences. However, their followers also created horrors like the Crusades, the Spanish Inquisition, anti-Semitic pogroms, and the cruelties of shariah law, to name only a few. Some other religions and cults have indulged in pointless atrocities like cannibalism and human sacrifice to curry the favor of mystic higher powers invented by human minds to explain the unknown and to exploit fear to rule their followers. Let it be clearly understood that none of these religions have anything to do with me. The universes are teeming with life-forms, but I have neither the desire nor an expectation of being worshiped by any of them, nor is it conceivable for me to listen to or respond to prayers. These, together with churches, temples, synagogues, and mosques, are harmless artifacts of religion and have no meaning beyond the notional comfort they may bring those who use them. Religions continue to be root sources of bitter hatreds, extremist followers, and atrocious acts conceived and perpetrated in their name.

Religious belief is frequently entwined with the philosophical concepts of good and evil, and corresponding value definitions of right and wrong. The deity in many personifications is often seen as the wellspring of good, and an opposing entity is imagined in the person of Satan, the devil, or other equivalent named manifestation. Good and evil, like religion, are entirely human conceptions. They have no absolute values and mean nothing in the absence of sentient societies. Picture a single being in isolation: nothing he can do could possibly be construed as either good or evil. He might do things which influence his own well-being or, alternatively, which are harmful to himself, but such actions are not philosophically good or evil. Higher meanings only become relevant in a society where the actions of an individual may have consequences for others. Religious leaders eventually adopted the expressions good and evil to describe collective effects of actions on their respective societies. You would do well to heed the wisdom inherent in the concepts of good and bad (evil is a dramatic word) as being relevant to human society but separate from any religious connotations.

It is a natural mechanism of primitive societies to develop mythical explanations to fill the gaps in their understanding of Nature. Many indeed are the folkloric stories of tribal history explaining the origins of human beings. The well-known biblical story of Adam and Eve is just one of many. The erstwhile frightening phenomenon of thunder and lightning exemplifies a natural occurrence conveniently explained in supernatural terms as "tools of the gods," and, even to this day, natural disasters are still referred to as "acts of God." As the frontier of human knowledge advances, mysteries are explained, and the fictions designed to comfort the ignorant become redundant. Unfortunately, another ugly side to religion is its extreme reluctance to give up on enshrined folklore, thereby perpetuating the inherent ignorance. The persistence of the doctrine of Creationism is an obvious example.

This, of course, leads into a subject dear to my heart (to use a strictly human expression). I would not say that I "created" your universe, or, for that matter, any of the many others that exist, but yes, I am responsible for their existence. There is a difference, which I will come back to a little later. Nonetheless, by making this statement, I am putting those of you who profess to be atheists on notice that you are mistaken. Some among you may argue that this letter is itself a work of fiction, but, please, do not expect me to indulge in miracles to convince you otherwise. Miracles of the biblical variety are not and have never been possible. Atheism is a courageous concept; as a statement of belief that there is no god, it implies knowledge of what God is. Certainly most of the traditional human conceptions of God can be argued to be faulty or inappropriate to modern thought and thus provide grist for the atheistic mill. However, your universe irrefutably exists, and therefore logic would have that it came into being somehow. The present state of your collective learning is completely inadequate to comprehend how or why this happened, and therefore it seems to be an immodest and presumptuous conclusion that there is no Creator.

Humans have biological limitations that make it very difficult for you to build an understanding of your universe. You are well able to sense and understand three physical dimensions and have a rudimentary concept of the significance of time. There are many more dimensions that are out of your field of perception and therefore hard for you to visualize in any way but as mathematical possibilities, much like your inability to visualize a color you have never seen, even though you are well aware of the ultraviolet and infrared spectra. Inexperience with more dimensions can be illustrated by the analogy of the ant. An ant is an insect with great strength for its size and weight, and therefore does not notice if it is moving uphill or down; it is essentially living in a two-dimensional world. Its field of perception is correspondingly small. Supposing intelligence was not a limiting factor, imagine the difficulty in explaining to an ant the significance of a mountain range or the depths of the oceans. Even harder to conceive would be bringing an ant to an understanding of a round world, space, or the solar system. No less of a problem is it for humans to understand their universe.

Nevertheless, you have made enormous advances in your knowledge, aided by the intuitive leaps of imagination of scientists like Albert Einstein, Stephen Hawking, and the pioneers of quantum theory. In a short time you have achieved a workable understanding of physics on both intergalactic and subnuclear scales. Your understanding of biological science has led you through great strides in disease control and agriculture, leading to longer and healthier lives and the ability to feed more and more of you as you proliferate your species. You have made these scientific advances in the very brief period since emerging from the Stone Age, and extrapolating your rate of progress millions of years into the future holds amazing possibilities, if you survive!

From experience with other races of beings in other parts of your universe as well as in other universes, I can tell you what you might be able to achieve and what you cannot achieve, but not whether you will achieve. The manufacturer of a pair of conventional dice can tell you it is impossible to roll more than twelve or less than two but cannot tell you what will be the outcome of a particular throw. Your future is not preordained but is completely yours alone to shape.

Creation

God speaks of His role in Creation and how life on Earth came about.

Your life experience, individually and collectively, has preconditioned you to believe in limits. Therefore you are uncomfortable with the concept of infinity, although you have defined it, and your mathematicians and physicists work with it. How can something have no beginning and no end? How can you visualize an entity so large that you can cut any amount off without making it any smaller or, alternatively, add to it without making it any larger? You are used to a world in which every effect has a cause, every physical entity has boundaries, and everything began at some point in time. These concepts are quite limiting in understanding the universe. You lean toward the thought that the universe had a beginning at some point in time, but if time itself did not exist at such a beginning, this becomes more an exercise in philosophy than in science.

Your scientists have proposed a model for the origin of the universe that you call the "big bang" theory. It postulates a definite moment in time when your universe started, from a tiny, dimensionless point (a "singularity," in mathematical jargon), from which it has been expanding ever since. The theory is silent on where this singularity came from or what surrounded it before the bang. Your scientists speculate on whether the laws of physics and the properties of matter were possibly varied during the early moments (measured in very small fractions of a second) of the bang. It has even been proposed that the force of gravity was briefly repulsive rather that attractive in those primordial moments.[1] My contribution in all of this was to formulate the laws of physics and how they apply to the interaction of energy and matter in a multidimensional environment. Once established, these laws are immutable and apply throughout all universes. You have

1 (Greene, 2004, 287-293)

devised models approximating the working of these laws at high speeds (relativity) and on a very small scale (quantum mechanics). Ultimately there will emerge the sought-after Unified Theory, the model that fits all circumstances, which will begin to approximate the truth. There is a long way to go and many hurdles to overcome to get there, including achieving a much better understanding of the true nature of time and other dimensions. There is yet much to learn about force fields and how they are created and transmitted and what determines their strength. The projected lifetime of your planet provides plenty of time for these studies, and as they progress you will conclude that the "big bang" theory is of little importance in the scheme of things. Your learning will eventually be vastly improved by biological breakthroughs in understanding the nature of knowledge itself in the chemistry of the human brain and how memory can be transmitted from one person to another and, indeed, preserved beyond the death of an individual.

Philosophers have pondered on what existed before the universe was created, and if it was the work of a Creator, where did this Creator come from and where was he then and where is he now? These are pure academic exercises in philosophy, and they presuppose that time existed before the universe was created so that "before" in this context actually has a meaning. Everything there is has always been in some form. This is not a trivial statement because it uses the word "always," which itself only has meaning in the context of the passage of time. As I have said earlier, you still have much to learn about the true nature of time. For example, you have recently learned that time is slowed down by gravitational fields and by travel at extremely high velocities.[2] If all of the matter in your "known" universe were concentrated in a singularity ahead of the "big bang," the gravitational field would conceivably be so strong that time would stand still—there would be no "before" and no "after," and so nothing would ever happen!

Earlier I said I was responsible for creation as opposed to being the "Creator." You might be surprised to know, in sharp contrast to most of your religious teachings, that I did not create life. Life abounds in all the universes and exists in innumerable forms and is simply one consequence of the laws of physics acting in the way I have designed them. Your physicists

2 (Hawking, 2010, 97-99, 133-134)

have learned that matter and energy are interchangeable and that your tangible world is essentially made up of three kinds of basic particles: protons, neutrons, and electrons. (Subcomponents of these are the subject of deeper studies.) The laws of physics govern how these particles interact with each other to make up atoms, of which there are some ninety-two stable kinds called elements. That is all, only ninety-two! Everything around you in your world consists of combinations of these relatively few types of atoms, which also follow the laws of physics to combine into what chemists call molecules. The molecules further combine with others to make chemical compounds of tremendous varieties, all in accordance with the action of the same laws of physics, facilitated by the ubiquitous presence of energy. Chemical compounds have a huge variety of physical properties. They can be solid, liquid, or gaseous; they can be hard, soft, brittle, flexible, shiny or dull, edible or poisonous, just to name a few. The huge variety of objects comprising your diverse surroundings, and indeed you yourselves, are all made up of those ninety-two building blocks.

On your planet, as elsewhere in the universe, a simple chemical compound of two gases, oxygen and hydrogen, is an odorless, tasteless, colorless, transparent liquid you call water. Water is an essential ingredient of all your life-forms and was instrumental in causing life on your planet to occur in the first instance. Water has truly remarkable physical properties (again, a consequence of the laws of physics!), one of which is that it is a very good solvent. Molecules of many different chemical compounds gain freedom to move about in solution, even if they may normally be solids or gases. Molecules suspended in liquids or ones dissolved in liquids move about randomly and, like bumper cars on a fairground, often collide with one another. The frequency and strength of collisions is dependent on the temperature of the liquid. Sometimes molecules of different compounds thus colliding in solution interact with each other and stick together, forming a new compound with different properties from those of the individual components. Anyone who has done high school chemistry experiments is familiar with this kind of process.

In the early millions of years in Earth's history, when water first formed and stayed on the surface—forming primordial pools, lakes, and oceans—many chemicals went into solution and had the opportunity to interact over hundreds of millions of years. Great stirrings occurred in the form of meteorite impacts, lightning strikes, storm activity, and tides. Temperature variations were frequent as the young planet cooled, and volcanic activity contributed hot upwellings of molten rock and more chemicals. Given this enormous length of time, eventually complex molecules were produced, which had an affinity for their own components, and so tended to grow in size until they broke apart, and then each part would grow again. Those molecules that could replicate themselves and thus populate their environment with like molecules using the components in their surroundings became the forerunners of life.

As more millions of years went by, random differences in their makeup caused some self-replicating molecules to become more successful than others in the competition for available materials, and so they developed more rapidly. The more successful ones tended to be more complex, benefiting from the synergy of variations in component parts to advance the capability of the whole. These became the first cells, which "fed" on their surroundings until reaching a certain size and then breaking up due to mechanical forces, with each new cell repeating the process. This evolution of cells happened haphazardly in many places on the young planet, and such cells were, not surprisingly, different from each other in countless ways. Many ran out of raw materials in their surrounding watery environment or suffered hostile changes in conditions and stopped growing. Eventually these became disassociated back into their original components, a process now described as "death." Others flourished long enough to gain in size and complexity, as random combinations of cells became more tolerant of changing surroundings and survived, while others failed. These were the first basic organisms. They happened by the working of physical laws that later became known as thermodynamics, mechanics, and electrostatics. These laws remain important in the field of chemistry, of which modern organic chemistry is an extension.

Another billion years went by, and more complicated organisms evolved by natural selection—as correctly interpreted by your scientist Darwin and others. The more successful ones were those that developed working combinations of speed of reproduction, size, ability to adapt to change, and ultimately, intelligence. The roots of intelligence began early on with the formation of cells that responded to outside stimuli with an internal movement of ions, constituting an electric current, and setting up an electric field that could influence neighboring cells. Such cells could respond by contracting and thereby contributing to a reactive movement of the organism. The advantage to an organism of being able to react to outside stimulus led to its greater success in a competitive environment. Such was the beginning of a nervous system and eventually of a rudimentary brain followed by development of senses for even more success in adaptation to external conditions.

Those of you who have tried to duplicate the creation of life in a laboratory have been unsuccessful, but that is not a reason to doubt the mechanism of its origin. What you call "abiogenesis" has taken billions of years and a vast range of extreme and changing conditions for the first life-forms to be generated, so do not expect to be able to replicate this with very limited knowledge in a very short time. There is no shortcut to evolution, which operates over many generations of even the most elementary organism within the environment it lives in. In this process the organism adapts and becomes hardened to survive in the presence of all surrounding factors, including cosmic radiation, microbiological symbiosis, surviving its own waste products, and competing for appropriate food, just to name some obvious ones. It is possible for humans eventually to reach a level of knowledge and ability to create new life-forms "in vitro," but these will not have the benefit of having coevolved in the external world environment, thus ensuring mutual symbiosis. If they become exposed to the outside they may not survive, but, on the other hand, such "aliens" may thrive with utterly disruptive and potentially disastrous consequences.

What has happened on your planet in its lifetime of some 4.5 billion years has, of course, happened elsewhere in your universe and all other universes, and is continuing to happen. In each case abiogenesis has produced life in forms shaped by individual physical environments in which a sufficient variety of chemicals have been exposed to each other in liquid surroundings and subjected to energy-rich turbulence. The same laws of physics apply everywhere, and the same ninety-two elements are the raw material. The randomness inherent in the process has resulted in the creation of a huge variety of life-forms with varying degrees of biological success. As they have on Earth, populations of beings have evolved, thrived, and collapsed, only to be replaced by others. The most widely successful creatures—measured by how long they have survived—are those who lived in complete harmony with their natural environment. In your case, for example, the dinosaurs survived for over one hundred million years. Their tenure as a successful species was ended only by their inability to survive a major natural catastrophe. Very few species have actually outlived the planet of their origin. Those that have are extremely intelligent and have developed the ability to control their own environment to a high degree. They have been able to advance their technologies and their knowledge to the level where they have successfully overcome their own weaknesses in order to work together with the common objective of racial survival. The human race could reach the threshold of such virtual immortality, if you persistently follow the path of learning you are now on. Earth will continue to exist for several billion more years—with or without you—so you have plenty of time, but you must survive to realize this possible destiny.

Survival

Humanity is on the edge of an uncertain future,
with a rough ride ahead.

I have emphasized the need for you to survive in order to realize the full potential of humanity. The forces against you are formidable, but by far the greatest are the adverse consequences of your own human nature. Your competitiveness and powerful tendency to act in your own personal self-interest are your evolutionary heritage, and they have driven you to the top of the food chain in your animal kingdom. Now that you are there, these traits can also become the cause of your undoing; they constitute the monster to be overcome on the journey into the future. Aside from the truly debilitating influence of religion, which promotes intellectual blindness and destructive prejudices, greed and hedonism are also characteristics with the most adverse potential.

Scientists have already learned by observation that any successful organism in a confined space—free of predation—will grow unchecked until it runs out of food or becomes poisoned by the abundance of its own waste. In either case, the result for the population is catastrophic. Higher life-forms in the terminal phase of such a situation typically turn on each other in the final struggle for survival. This is a critical lesson. The success of human beings has allowed them to overpopulate the planet to the extent that starvation is widespread in spite of enormous advances in agriculture. Millions of people are living in lands that cannot support them by indigenous food production. Humanitarian aid, well-intentioned as it may be, is unfortunately not a viable long-term answer. Most aid does not provide a permanent solution, and therefore only serves to postpone the inevitable course of Nature. At the same time, your industries catering to the insatiable desire for consumer goods of those with disposable income are polluting the atmosphere and diminishing the available supply of potable water. Millions of people suffer from very limited access to clean drinking water and adequate sanitary provisions. The immodest consumption of energy by the affluent is causing massive pollution and an escalating depletion of global resources. This is not the picture of a sustainable future.

Tragically, you do not have the political will or strength of leadership capable of mandating and enforcing global change on a scale that can avert the natural consequences that will otherwise certainly overtake you. How these natural forces will play out is not foreseeable, inevitable as the outcome must be. The result, however, will be a massive reduction in the population, at least to a number that the planet can easily sustain. What this number will be and the quality of life for those that remain will be determined by their ability to live in harmony with the environment at a self-sustaining level of consumption.

The preferred source of the impending change would be a gradual, worldwide decline in population driven by a lower birth rate and attrition in regions least capable of sustaining life. A more probable alternative is the advent of a natural catastrophe, most likely in the form of a deadly pandemic. Physical events, such as the impact of a meteorite or a climate changing volcanic eruption, are not without precedent, but those would be coincidental and not caused by the population crisis that will otherwise give rise to its own solution. Such events could be terminal, as it was for the population of dinosaurs in Earth's distant past. The probability of cataclysmic events is low, and may not loom until distant future inhabitants have developed the capability of predicting and perhaps dealing with such threats. The remaining catalyst for change could be the escalation of hostilities between humans with nuclear, biological, or other weapons of mass destruction. At least that is an alternative within your capability to avoid, except for acts of terrorism motivated by religious extremism.

A significant decline in world population will be a drastic but essential occurrence, and it will not be endured without suffering that will attend forced correction of the excesses of the present age. Natural forces will not be halted by sentiment. Earth will survive completely indifferent to the life-forms it hosts from time to time. It will move on in its destiny of billions of years with or without humans. Whether your descendents are there as long as the great lizards were, or even until the final geological era of the planet, depends upon the ability of the human spirit to adapt and to allow intelligence to rule over the primitive urges of your nature.

Whether change comes upon the human race by cataclysm or by orderly reconfiguration, it will bring massive economic changes for the survivors, principally in the production and distribution of food and in the generation and use of energy. The disruption in the way of life may be large and long-lived, but in the end, the possibility is there for the opening of new frontiers in science and technology. Evolution has equipped you with a powerful brain, the extent of whose capability has not yet been imagined.

Unlimited Potential

Great benefits can come from further technological advances.

As I have disappointed the atheists among you, I must also disappoint the fatalists, those who think the future is predetermined by an all-powerful deity, as well as those who believe that a "higher power" has an influence over events that have not yet happened. I return to the simple analogy of the pair of dice; their manufacturer can tell you with certainty the maximum and minimum count that can result from a roll of the dice, but he cannot foresee the outcome of any individual roll or sequence of rolls. The laws of physics are immutable and ubiquitous, and they determine without exception how matter and energy are interchangeable and react in all forms and circumstances. This letter is not intended to teach physics or to preempt your own research into the secrets of Nature. Your capacity for learning is enormous, and your understanding will grow at your own pace with the fullness of time. The laws of physics set the only limit on what the future may bring. My audience is intended to be as wide as possible, and therefore is not limited to those who have an advanced technical education.

The past century, which is but a tiny flash in geological time—related to the age of Earth—has seen an impressive explosion in human knowledge and technology. This has been fuelled by a combination of factors, including more candidates for higher education, more funding for research, industrial and military competition, and the deployment of advanced tools, such as computers (themselves a product of the technology explosion). These prolific scientific advances have contributed to enhanced food production, disease reduction, and longevity, as well as stunning improvements in communications and mobility. Collaterally, they have also produced world-threatening weapons of mass destruction and the means to deliver them. They have fallen behind badly in capacity to deal with unwanted consequences like waste disposal, pollution, and energy consumption. A vast majority of humans have not benefited from the technological advances. In many parts of the world life expectancy remains relatively short; starvation and poverty affect more people than ever; local wars persist, fuelled by fanaticism and hatred, and, importantly, the average level of human happiness has not kept pace.

The exponential growth in learning and technology is nearing its end. The demographic reasons have been discussed already, but another reason is that the educational process is reaching a plateau. Scientists who wish to achieve the cutting edge of knowledge in their chosen fields must already spend a great portion of their most productive years studying in order to catch up with the advanced state of their art. This is because each human being comes into the world with no knowledge and must start learning from the very beginning. At the other end of life, the most experienced and knowledgeable people take what they know to the grave, and it is forever lost. More and more knowledge is being archived electronically in readily accessible form, which is a partial solution. However, in the future it will be learned how knowledge and memory are stored in the human brain and how they can be replicated and transferred to another person without the recipient having to endure the otherwise laborious and costly learning process entailed in a classical education. Once this is achieved, scientists in the prime of their creative years will be ready to work with the full suite of knowledge of their predecessors available directly to their thought processes. As such new power is ready to be deployed, great new advances can occur again, and in a world with a smaller and stable population, great benefits can be realized.

You are still a long way from realizing the full potential of computers. Memories and computing power will increase as the physical size of components continues to shrink to the molecular level. Improvement in reliability and reduction in unit costs will ensure their wider use in every aspect of daily life. Voice recognition, face recognition, DNA analysis, and basic medical diagnostics will become accurate, fast, and cheap, with obvious benefits.

Advances in microbiology and nanobiology will be equally spectacular. The construction of altered special-purpose cells will expedite the creation of vaccines, which will eventually be bypassed as the technology for direct synthesis of specific-purpose antibodies becomes practical. Injected and swallowed microcomputer capsules or tiny, externally controlled robots with communication capability will greatly enhance medical diagnoses and localized administration of drugs. The problem of rejection in organ transplants will be overcome, and increased repair capability of damaged organs will reduce the need for transplants in a majority of cases. Geriatric science will be able to make vast inroads into relieving the debilitating effects of aging. Cures will be found eventually for diabetes and cancers, as well as for obesity. A lot of these medical breakthroughs will come in conjunction with a better understanding of the human brain and how it controls bodily functions and performance. The end result will be a great increase in the human life span, particularly the length of time humans will remain fit, productive, and capable of enjoying a high quality of life. This will make up for a voluntary reduced birthrate and a low but stable population.

Notwithstanding great medical advances, the world will never be free of disease. The nature of evolution and the breeding cycle of the vectors of malady will constantly deliver new permutations of disease carriers, viral and bacterial. Their presence and effect must be diagnosed, which does not happen before they have made themselves felt through sickness of the host. It will always be a challenge for medicine to stay ahead of these new strains and neutralize them effectively.

There will no longer be a need for humans to scrabble for survival in barren parts of the world or places with harsh climates. Further spectacular advances in communication and entertainment will reduce the demand for travel, particularly for business, thus greatly easing the pressure on transportation at every level, from municipal to international. When travel is necessary or desired, it will be faster, safer, and more comfortable. Transportation of raw materials from their sources and finished goods from factories to consumers, as well as transportation of foodstuffs, will be largely automated and unobtrusive.

Free from the crushing pressure of overpopulation and the great economic burden of supporting and deploying an unproductive military machine, human beings may once again face the challenge of venturing into interplanetary space and advancing their understanding of the visible universe. They will achieve colonies on the moon and on Mars. They will greatly improve their propulsion systems and will experience manned visits to other parts of the solar system. They will learn amazing things about Jupiter and Saturn and their moons, but human beings will not travel to the stars.

In a readjusted world all these things are possible, and not in the least improbable. There is however, a caveat. As mentioned earlier, human beings have innate characteristics that have helped them to the top of the evolutionary heap. These include aggressive self-interest and basic greed. Can people stand prosperity? Can they govern themselves without rancor? How long before the venal side of human nature reasserts itself to cause renewed disharmony? Your history is against you. The cycle in which prosperity leads to proliferation, territorialism, and conflict could repeat itself with similar consequences. The planet will survive, but will the human race?

The potential for a positive outcome and an exciting future remains there for you to realize.

Energy

The pattern of human energy consumption can and must change.

Living requires energy. The working of the brain itself and the voluntary and involuntary muscles of the body all consume energy. Until very recently on a geological scale, the energy fueling life came from consumption of food that directly captured it from the sun. Then the development of machinery created a huge new demand for energy to deliver power and speed to human endeavors. Population of otherwise inhospitable climate zones produced new demands for heat and air conditioning as humans sought artificially comfortable surroundings. Availability of coal and hydrocarbons obliged, and the greatly increased requirement for energy to fuel a new, industrialized world was readily satisfied.

The carbon-rich fossil fuels that have been so accommodating took many millions of years to form, and their supply is limited. In addition, their combustion products are not part of the natural climate cycle that has characterized Earth for millions of years. In the quantities now being produced, fossil fuel by-products are distorting the atmospheric balance of the planet with life-changing consequences. You have now reached an unsustainable pattern of energy consumption, and changes will be forced upon you in the near future.

Fortunately, your planet has been blessed with a virtually unlimited source of clean energy, the same as that which fuels the stars. Thermonuclear fusion can occur between isotopes of hydrogen available in water. This is a form of nuclear reaction that has the potential to provide you with all the energy you will ever need, once you discover the technology to control it—as opposed to making hydrogen bombs. You will find that this form of energy, released as heat, will be generated in large stationary facilities that will use it to produce electricity. In order to extend its use to transportation, you will need to develop far more efficient and portable energy storage technology. This too will happen and finally free you from your voracious appetite for fossil fuels. You will never be free from the need for oil, but with unlimited electrical power, you will be able to re-create oil from water and carbon dioxide, thereby neutralizing the polluting effect of burning such oil in the first place.

Time

Time is still a concept that is hard for humans to grasp.

Time is the least understood of the dimensions within your perception. You see it as homogenous and unstoppable and as the separator between cause and effect. It is the invisible ocean within which your universe appears to be unfolding. Exciting progress has yet to be made in gaining a fuller understanding of time, of its workings, and its role in the operation of the laws of physics.

Time travel has always been a popular subject for your science fiction writers, but it is not a real possibility in the glamorous sense they like to portray. There are logical prohibitions to travel into the past that also apply to returning from trips to the future. Of course, everybody is constantly traveling into the future at the same rate, and indeed the "present" is only a fleeting boundary between the past and the future. Locating the present in three-dimensional space can become confusing. For example, suppose that at a moment considered to be the present time at a point A in space, an event takes place. At another point, B, physically distant from A, that event remains in the future for the length of time it takes light to travel from point A to point B. If you find this strange, it serves to show that understanding time is not as easy as you may wish.

There is no physical prohibition to travel into the future, but it can only be done by isolating the traveler from the effect of the passage of time, and allowing time to flow past until the target point in the future is reached. A "time capsule" is a simple example of this. Before it can be done by a living being, the art of suspended animation must be perfected. Limited travel into the future can also be achieved by travel at relativistic speeds—traveling at close to the speed of light—but that is not usefully practical! Clearly no such trip is reversible, allowing the traveler to return.

Space Travel and Aliens

Other intelligent beings exist but humans will not meet them.

The laws of physics do not preclude travel to and from other star systems or even other galaxies. However, the problems of living beings doing so are enormous, and the dangers are formidable, to the extent that cost will always exceed the need. The limiting factor is sheer distance. Life-forms evolved to live in the presence of planetary gravity are not able to withstand substantially higher forces for long periods of time, and therefore the magnitude of acceleration for "manned" vehicles is limited. This means long periods of acceleration to reach a meaningful fraction of the speed of light and similar periods of deceleration at journey's end. Even the shortest interstellar trip is therefore a matter of many years.

By the time the technology is developed for you to have that capability, you will have solved so many more local problems that travel to the stars will not receive practical consideration. The idea of saving the human race in the dying days of your solar system is a science fiction fantasy that will be long forgotten by that time. The end of life on your planet will be a long and slow process over many generations, with diminishing populations as conditions gradually become less favorable. There will be no fearful rush for the exit.

For the same reasons there have been no visits to Earth from aliens representing far advanced civilizations, nor will there be in the future. Such advanced civilizations are those who have also learned to live in sustainable harmony with their native surroundings within their own planetary systems. They certainly exist, and eventually you will find evidence of this, but communication with them will never become a reality because of the huge length of time for a reply to be returned and a vast cultural and linguistic barrier. You will eventually have greater success communicating effectively with other living species on your own planet.

Predicting the Future

What can and what cannot be foreseen.

The future on a grand scale is determined by the interaction of matter and energy in your universe in accordance with the laws of physics. A system is in motion that is far more complex than you will ever realize or even imagine. Go back to the analogy of a pair of dice; they have been manufactured and thrown, and while they are rolling, the outcome is undetermined and unpredictable within the limits built into them. So it is on a cosmic scale. On the nearer term, a clear understanding of the laws of physics allows a degree of success in prediction of future events. For example, your understanding of the motion of the planets and their satellites allows you to predict solar and lunar eclipses and the return of orbiting comets with impressive precision. Your ability to predict the tidal ebb and flow of your oceans is highly accurate, as is your ability to calculate the trajectories of missiles, artificial satellites, and missions to other planets. On the other hand, your ability to forecast the weather is rudimentary, and your ability to predict earthquakes is nonexistent. Why?

To make any worthwhile prediction, you must have a complete knowledge of all the elements that influence the system for which a future is to be foretold and know how each is affected by the laws of Nature. Of course, you must begin with a complete knowledge of the state of all these elements at the beginning (starting conditions). Approximations can often work for short-term predictions, but inaccuracies quickly become magnified by the passage of time. Weather forecasting is a prime example. The prediction that it is not going to rain in the afternoon can be quite reliable if the starting condition is a clear blue sky in the morning. A five-day forecast requires far more knowledge of the starting conditions over a much larger area. So many factors affect the weather that even the most powerful computers can only give an approximate forecast over a relatively short time period.

Prediction of earthquakes is impossible without a complete assessment of starting conditions deep below the surface of the planet. You are still a long way from being able to achieve this. As systems become more complicated, usually through the large number of contributing elements, prediction can become impossible—such as predicting when and where the next lightning strike will take place in a thunderstorm. All the physical principles involved in this are very well known, but the details of atmospheric substructure at any moment are far too complex to be tractable.

Other systems that appear to be disarmingly simple are nevertheless impossible to predict. Come back to the roll of dice referred to earlier. This sort of system can be analyzed by applying the laws of probability, which also play a great role in evolutionary development in biology.

Long-term prediction of the future of a system involving living components with intelligence and free will is an impossible undertaking, even from the point of view of experience with other populations in other parts of this and other universes. Where a biological system is physically contained in a confined space, namely the surface of Earth, one outcome is certain. The population must become adjusted to the ability of the planet to sustain it. There are a number of ways in which this boundary condition can be met, as inevitably it will be. One is the decline of the population in an orderly fashion, and another is a decline by catastrophe. The latter may be difficult to control and could lead to a third possible outcome: a decline of the population to zero. This suite of possibilities has been raised earlier in this letter and is repeated here to emphasize the importance of realizing that you must act now or face the consequences. Mother Nature does not have a kind heart, and I do not interfere with orderly unfolding of the universes.

Other Dimensions

Our senses are not able to perceive
all the dimensions of the universe.

At the beginning of this letter, I pointed out that your biological limitations create great difficulties in your ability to understand your universe. These limitations are: inability to perceive more than the four dimensions of space-time and difficulty in conceptualizing an absence of limits. The latter makes it hard for you to visualize infinities in space and time. (You are predisposed to believe entities must have physical boundaries and have a beginning and an end.) Dealing with other dimensions is much harder still (remember the analogy of the ant). The reality is that the universe exists in many more dimensions than the four you can easily perceive. The mathematical equations you have developed to describe the laws of physics are mostly reduced to solutions in the four familiar dimensions of space-time and are quite successful in explaining what you see happening. Only recently have your physicists attempted to include up to nine spatial dimensions, plus time as a tenth, in highly sophisticated attempts to develop the ultimate Unified Theory[3]. They are on the right track.

The problem you face is working in a space defined by fewer dimensions than exist in reality. The difficulty is not unlike having to work entirely with shadows cast on a two-dimensional wall in order to develop physical laws governing happenings in three dimensions.

Everything around you exists in all of the dimensions of the universe, but is only visible to you in three dimensions plus time. A complete description of reality would require identifying all coordinates in all of the dimensions, with motion being described by changes over time of any or all of them. This represents a near-impossibility for you. The ability to advance your knowledge to the extent you have is only possible because you mostly seek

---

3 (Greene, 2004, 359)

answers in the visible portion of your environment; the approximation of ignoring the other dimensions works well within this constraint. In the section on predicting the future, an additional complicating feature is the extent to which the effects of a fuller, multidimensional reality must be taken into account.

A Spirit World?

Phenomena and effects related to the existence of other dimensions.

Your literature and folklore are rich in references to an "afterlife," a soul, the existence of spirits, haunting, near-death experiences, and even references to "past lives" evoked by hypnotic regression[4]. There remains a widespread belief in telepathy, fortune-telling, astrology, Karma, and other nonmedical influences on the human condition. This whole subject represents an aspect of the current boundary between what can and what cannot be explained by the laws of Nature as you now know them. Over the ages, this boundary has steadily been pushed back as scientific knowledge has advanced. This process will continue. Some ancient beliefs have been permanently dispelled, such as the alchemist's quest to turn lead into gold and the existence of a "fountain of youth." However, the fact that seemingly inexplicable phenomena can eventually be explained by science does not mean that such phenomena no longer exist. Your ability to explain thunder and lightning in scientific terms does not make them go away!

As with everything else, biological systems evolved and exist in all the dimensions of the universe. As they become more complex, they are more deeply embedded in the full multidimensional environment and the more they are affected by forces acting in the unseen dimensions. In no case is this truer than in humans themselves. The human brain represents the pinnacle of evolutionary achievement to the present day. One of the greatest challenges of modern medicine is diagnosis and treatment of maladies that are rooted in dimensions not directly visible. The symptoms are like the shadows on the wall referred to above and, consequently, are as difficult to treat. The brain exercises control of the host body on a

---

4 (Weiss, 1988)

multidimensional level, including a spectrum of ailments and healing processes medical science refers to as psychosomatic. For example, there is no connection in the three-dimensional world between a placebo and the patient, yet often placebos are effective. The connection is there in other dimensions.

Human perception of the world outside the body occurs by impulses transmitted to the brain by sensory organs, most importantly the eyes. Because the brain is the product of billions of years of evolution in a multidimensional environment, it is possible for it to recognize messages transmitted to it in a wider range than perceived by the classical five senses. Evolution did not equip the body with obvious sensors able to "see" in more than three dimensions. However, that does not preclude certain individuals having an above-average capacity to assimilate multidimensional information, some even to a substantial degree. It would be abnormal for this not to be the case. Such people have been recognized as having a "sixth sense," or ESP (extrasensory perception). In some cases, these individuals have developed an understanding of the information thus available to them, and they can use it beneficially. These people in ancient times were called "seers," "oracles," or "prophets," and their powers were popularly ascribed to contact with the appropriate deities of the time. In other societies or at other times ESP powers were referred to as "witchcraft," and those so empowered were widely feared and even punished. Today, such people are said to have "psychic" powers. Such powers are limited by the degree to which extrasensory information is received and by the ability of the receiver to recognize and process it intelligently. Psychics are still marginalized by the mainstream population. The science is not yet understood; the powers vary, and those with such capabilities are skeptically regarded as "mystics" and mostly lumped together with fringe players claiming connections to the world of the occult.

The science of ESP is in its infancy, but it represents a doorway to explore the significance of other dimensions in living organisms as well is in theories of physics. There are diseases that you barely understand and for which you consequently have difficulty in finding a cure, such as Alzheimer's, Parkinson's, multiple sclerosis, ALS, and most forms of cancer. The reason is that their roots are multidimensional, and so, to some extent, medical science is working on their shadows in the three-dimensional world. While it is not impossible to hit upon causes and cures for intractable diseases in the course of conventional medicine, improved ESP capability will prove to be an invaluable tool in the future. The multidimensional capacity of the brain must become better understood and harnessed for humanity to reach its full potential.

Life beyond Life

A form of immortality.

This has been a long letter, given to you at a crucial time in your existence. It is not intended to assist you in your quest for a better understanding of Nature. You have much to discover, but evolution has equipped you with a brain capable of great learning and imagination. It is, however, a warning that your survival is at stake. The human race has bloomed and spread across the surface of your planet like a virulent rash, consuming everything in its path. This will not end well, as it is a progression that will inevitably run out of sustenance and drown in its own waste. A voluntary curb to unsustainable population growth is possible and is not yet out of your reach. Earth will continue to exist for billions of years, regardless of any human presence. The probability is still good that your race will survive, but in greatly reduced numbers, and hopefully will be rid of the destructive elements that have plagued its past. Earlier I dismissed the word "evil" as being too dramatic, but I will use it here: religion, racism, and greed are the evils that can be the destroyers of your civilization.

I will end with a positive note. Life is not over with the death of a physical body existing in three dimensions. Life, which is a highly complex result of the working of evolution in all of the dimensions of the universe, can continue to exist in the remaining dimensions after loss of its three-dimensional component. You have experienced and recognized some evidence of this, and the implications will give scientists in your future a fertile field of study in the search for better knowledge of your universe.

[End of the letter]

Discussion

Opium of the Masses

"Religion is the opium of the masses."—Karl Marx

God exists, but religion is an artifact of the human mind.

There can be no doubt that God exists. What is meant by this statement is, of course, centered on the definition of "exists." God, in multiple forms and names has certainly been prevalent in human thinking since before recorded history, and hundreds of millions of people are believers in one form or another. Such belief is formalized in the literature and practice of the world's major religions. Even though these religions conflict in many and often hostile ways, the common thread of a revered deity is significant. Such entrenchment in the human psyche is not easily waived off as coincidence. This has led some philosophers to conjecture that we are "hardwired" to seek and believe in a higher power, and that this is intended to bring us to the realization of the deity. Without needing to touch upon the philosophy of truth, the ubiquitous presence of God in the minds of so many for so long is in itself a definition of existence.

So, as recipients of the letter, how shall we react? The overwhelming initial interpretation will be highly skeptical. Religion is under attack, and religious groups driven by the ponderous momentum of centuries will not suffer lightly any suggestion that they are on a wrong track. Similarly, atheists and agnostics may not easily give up their reasoned beliefs as honed by their life's thoughts and experiences. After all, the letter is no different from any other "revelation" that cannot be substantiated. So we must judge it on its content, even if skeptics dispute its source.

It is impossible to argue against the thesis that religion has, and continues to have, a negative influence on humanity. History is too long interwoven with strife and suffering caused by the drive of believers to convert others to their way of thought, almost always with virulent intolerance of freedom of choice. Global unrest to this day is largely centered on terrorism for which responsibility is frequently claimed by fundamentalist religious factions. The economic cost and inconvenience of protecting civilization from suicide attacks has become egregious in the extreme. Simple logic dictates that all religions cannot be right, and if most of them are flawed, probably all are. However, they have survived through the ages. Why?

As the letter says, religion has also served a useful purpose, in that adept leaders of men have used the power of superstition to motivate their peoples into acceptable social behavior. The dissemination of the Ten Commandments by Moses is a prime example. Indeed, many religions have common ground in formulating the mores of living together. The success of the spiritual element to clothe rules that are basic common sense has been greatest among primitive societies with little education. In such environments, religion offers hope and comfort to followers of those taking leadership. However, it is the perpetuation of spiritual trappings that comes into increasing conflict with expanding scientific knowledge.

As is so often the case, the main culprit in this dispute is ignorance. Hard facts define the boundary between faith and knowledge. Arguments with those who deny factual evidence that refutes their beliefs are hard to win. Such is the difficulty in defusing the debate on replacement of creationism by the theory of evolution. As time passes and the frontiers of knowledge expand, the case for evolutionary development is becoming ever more compelling. The letter clearly supports this position.

The concept of God originates in the dim, distant past of humanity and is surprisingly ubiquitous. Perhaps it originates in the atavistic need for guidance and comfort that seems to be a part of our psyche. Human beings have a definite herd instinct that predisposes us to follow charismatic leaders. This has been exploited through the ages by the likes of Genghis Khan, Julius Caesar, Napoleon, and Adolf Hitler. It is a characteristic that can lead to mass hysteria and is seldom a force for the common good. All of these notorious leaders have been the cause of legendary bloodshed, highlighting the bizarre fact that humans, while the most intelligent creatures on Earth, are the only ones who regularly and mercilessly kill each other in large numbers.

Another impetus for seeking a deity is our reluctance to come to grips with the unknown. God provides an easy answer to such puzzling questions as where we came from, why, and what for? He also provides a handy scapegoat to accept blame for disasters large or small, whether it is the untimely loss of a loved one or a natural catastrophe. The letter recognizes these roots of religion but is clear on only one issue—creation of the rules governing the interaction of energy and matter in the unfolding of the universe. The message of the letter is that these rules themselves are not a random event. Perhaps that is the single most important message, and one that represents a fundamental challenge to atheism.

Writers of letters inevitably tell us about themselves, and in this case God is clearly distancing himself from continuing involvement in that which he has set in motion, and in particular involvement with us, to whom the letter is addressed. Prayers, religious rites, and ecclesiastical buildings are all cast as human-inspired artifacts strictly for the benefit of those using them. The "merciful God," to whom prayers are frequently intoned, is not, as must be apparent to anyone witnessing man's inhumanity to man in times of war, including the too frequent perpetration of genocide. When both sides in a conflict claim God is on their side, they cannot seriously expect anything beyond the comfort of wishful thinking!

The rise of human intelligence above the level predominant in the rest of the animal kingdom has only been extremely recent on the scale of geological time. Awareness of the vastness of the universe and our insignificant place in it has been even more recent. It is not surprising that this new knowledge has not yet had much impact on the fabric of religious belief. The writers of the scriptures upon which most religions are still based, as well as the subjects of their work, were very ignorant of natural science by today's standards. The early ideas that we were the center of everything and made in the image of God now seem monstrously immodest, and yet changes in religious thinking do not seem imminent.

The message of the letter is unambiguous: our survival is in the balance, and to save ourselves we will have to unite in our approach to live in harmony with our planet.

Oil Is Forever and the Energy Race

Our usage and sources of energy will determine our lifestyle.

When the history of mankind is finally written, the present age will no doubt be dubbed the Oil Age. As we rose from the Stone Age through the Bronze Age and the Iron Age, these demarcations became plain as new technologies created new ways of life. Those earlier ages gave us newer materials to make better tools (and weapons) that helped humans on their relentless climb toward domination of their environment.

Perhaps more significant to the rise of the human animal above other creatures was the ability to harness energy. This began with the discovery of fire, or, more particularly, how to control and use fire for warmth, cooking, protection, and later for winning metals from their ores. Taming the flame allowed not only the production of iron but its transformation into steel (more, better weapons). Not unrelated was the advancement of chemistry, and the early discovery that heat speeds up chemical reactions. The invention of gunpowder and other explosives, while peripherally useful for other purposes, mainly produced another escalation in the destructive capability of weapons.

The leap in the use of energy fuelled the Industrial Revolution, which can be taken as the starting point of modern times. The prodigious burning of coal also initiated the collateral rise to awareness of air pollution, which resulted in the notorious "pea soup" fogs of London, and that is still so evident in the debilitating smogs in Eastern Europe and China.

The latest great escalation in the consumption of energy came with the discovery of oil and its impact on transportation, aided by development of the internal combustion engine. Oil has made the automobile and air travel a way of modern life, and its profligate use awakened in us the fear of global warming. Oil and natural gas together have spawned a civilization dangerously dependent on hydrocarbons for its standard of living. Not only are we dependent on this fuel for transportation, but as feedstock for a giant petrochemical industry supplying such taken-for-granted products as plastics and fertilizers.

The letter gives us a clear warning about our future. The capabilities of the human brain and ingenuity have been amply demonstrated in the exponential explosion of technology. While the potential seems unlimited, that is not Nature's way. Limits will occur, for no progression can go indefinitely unchecked. This is particularly true of the planet's human population and its thirst for oil. Even though it may not all have been discovered yet, the world's reserves of oil are finite, as is its ability to grow food. It is self-evident that the growth in human population must end, and end soon. The spectrum of starvation already looms large in too many regions, and dense populations are severely vulnerable to the spread of disease and the impact of other natural disasters. The letter does not offer us a solution; nor is one clearly apparent.

The old saw says that the Stone Age did not end because of a lack of stone. Far in the future it will be acknowledged that Earth did not run out of oil. Over the short term, the economic law of supply and demand will limit consumption by making petroleum products less affordable as natural sources dwindle. Without question, this will be accompanied by severe disruptions in standards of living, particularly among the highest users of energy. The good news is that this is a problem that may be solved.

One reason that the dinosaurs survived on this planet for 150 million years was that their existence was in a harmonious energy balance with their environment. Many were large and needed a lot of energy to move around, but they obtained it directly from eating vegetation and indirectly by eating each other, thereby utilizing resources daily renewed by solar energy through photosynthesis in a massive plant-rich ecosystem. The rate at which they could use energy was limited by the power of their muscles and by how fast recovery could be fuelled by the working of their digestive systems. These natural processes were slow and indefinitely sustainable.

Similarly, for all but the tiny, most recent fraction of their existence on Earth, humans were limited in their consumption of energy. Up until the Industrial Revolution in the nineteenth century, humans were unable to travel any faster than the speed of a horse. Animal muscle power set a natural speed limit throughout history until the invention of the steam engine forever changed the dynamics of human existence. It is the transportation explosion that has redefined our relationship with the environment and that has launched us into dangerous energy imbalance. In barely two centuries, we have progressed from transcontinental wagon train migrations to mass global air travel at close to the speed of sound. People who, a few generations ago, could not think of moving faster than an Arabian steed, now see manned space stations orbiting Earth every few hours. All this became possible as we learned to concentrate the use of large amounts of energy over short time frames, a prodigious application of power.

Power is defined as the rate at which energy is delivered. A commonly used measure of power is the watt—named after a pioneer inventor of the steam engine. A (now old-fashioned) incandescent domestic lightbulb uses energy at a rate of 100 watts, and a hot plate on a kitchen stove on a high setting uses about 1,000 watts. Today's automobiles are still rated in terms of horsepower (hp). A so-called "muscle car" of 350 hp at peak performance uses over a quarter of a million watts, the equivalent of burning twenty-five hundred light bulbs at once. Let us look at this in comparison to the energy of the sun falling on the surface of Earth: the annual average solar power per square meter of the planet's surface is about 240 watts. The muscle car driver with the pedal to the metal is therefore using energy at the rate being delivered to us by the sun over an area of over one thousand square meters!

Moving up the scale, the peak power required by a modern jetliner during takeoff is approximately 200 million watts (commonly written 200 MW, for megawatts), generated by burning jet fuel at a rate of approximately 16,000 kg per hour, the equivalent to the average solar power falling onto some 833,000 square meters of Earth's surface. There is only one way known today of concentrating that much energy in such a local and mobile place, and that is through the combustion of oil. Roughly one third of the energy consumption in the Western world is related to mobility, which has become a fundamental factor in the global economy. Only a very few generations ago people were born, lived, and died in local communities. Now we travel around the world for business and pleasure in huge numbers and consume products manufactured halfway around the globe on a daily basis. Human beings are no longer living in sustainable harmony with their environment. A solution must be found, and the letter makes clear that our survival and preservation of our present standard of living depends on our ability to do so.

The amount of energy stored in a liter of gasoline is far greater than that possible in any state-of-the-art battery, at a small fraction of the weight, including the container (tank). For example, one liter of gasoline, weighing 0.73 kg, contains approximately five times the amount of available energy from a 50 kg lead-acid golf cart battery. This comparison is significant when it comes to alternative methods of powering transportation, in which weight and volume are both critical.

The current method of storing electrical energy (in batteries) is far behind the chemical alternative represented by petroleum. For instance, a compact car, which has a 100 kw power unit (134 hp), can be driven by a 400 kg nickel metal hydride battery, which typically releases the same amount of energy as three liters of gasoline. The battery would be quickly drained at full power but would last several hours at low cruising power. The concept of large-scale use of electric automobiles is a marginal proposition. Even the most advanced battery technology provides a low energy yield at high cost compared to gasoline. The supposed improvement in the reduction of air pollution by electric cars over petroleum-powered vehicles is largely imaginary. Why? Because the electricity needed to recharge the batteries is mostly generated from burning fossil fuels! If this is to change, the energy capacity of electrical storage devices needs to be improved by at least a hundredfold, so that clean energy sources like wind farms can store energy in portable containers for later, remote uses. This is a critical technological breakthrough that must be prioritized by human ingenuity.

While huge advances in electrical energy storage technology might make electrical automobiles more realistic, the prodigious need for power required to lift jetliners into the sky makes the future of electric aircraft a most unlikely prospect. The energy concentration and portability of jet fuel is so vastly superior to other alternatives that it is most likely to remain the sole propellant of air travel far into the future. So, what happens if the supply runs out?

Again, it will be up to human ingenuity to engineer the solution, which is one that is theoretically within our reach: the thermonuclear alternative. The energy contained in one kg of ordinary water, in terms of the raw material for the hydrogen fusion reaction, is equivalent to almost eight hundred liters of gasoline. This is the nuclear reaction that fuses two heavy hydrogen nuclei together to form helium, accompanied by the release of a lot of energy. This reaction fuels the sun (and the hydrogen bomb) and produces no radioactive waste, unlike the uranium fission that fuels conventional nuclear power plants. The difficulty is in being able to initiate, contain, and control the fusion reaction in order to harness the energy generated. Once this can be done, the supply of energy becomes virtually unlimited and clean.

The technical problem with controlling nuclear fusion is that extremely high temperatures are needed to initiate and maintain the reaction. This is required to overcome the very strong electrostatic repulsive force that works to keep the hydrogen nuclei apart. They must be forced very close together before the much stronger, but short-range, nuclear force can operate to fuse them into helium and release the desired energy. That is why a conventional atomic (fission) bomb is used to trigger the far more devastating hydrogen bomb. The reaction temperatures are so high that material containment vessels would be vaporized. Experimental work is proceeding using magnetic fields for containment, but much progress is still needed. The concept of "cold fusion," as promised by a recent hoax, is not a scientific possibility.

The world that has succeeded in harnessing this source of energy will look very different indeed. Most importantly, it will no longer rely on the extraction of fossil fuels from the ground. That will herald the end of coal mining and offshore oil drilling and open the door to dealing with the dreaded carbon footprint reviled by today's environmentalists. Strangely, it will do this without the need to end the reliance of the transportation industry on petroleum-based fuels to provide the power density needed for air travel. This can be made to happen by the advent of synthetic petroleum products made by combining water with carbon dioxide extracted from the atmosphere. Not only does this remove that so-called greenhouse gas from the environment, but it also returns oxygen, as is the case with photosynthesis—indeed a process in harmony with Nature.

Work has already been done on artificial petroleum using hydrogen electrolyzed from seawater combined with carbon dioxide dissolved in the ocean to synthesize hydrocarbons. Research is also being conducted at the Clean Energy Research Centre at the University of British Columbia using solar energy and catalysts to break down carbon dioxide in the presence of water to produce usable fuels. Such processes are highly energy intensive, because the energy released in the original burning of the hydrocarbon fuel must be put back. This desirable objective of carbon recycling ought to become practical in the presence of an unlimited energy source. With petroleum remaining the most efficient method of storing great quantities of energy, further ingenuity will certainly continue to be expended to perfect the recapture of its combustion products for recombination into new fuel. In this way there is a foreseeable path for technology to return us to an undiminished and sustainable energy balance.

The Mystery of Time

Einstein once said that the flow of time prevents everything from happening at once.

The letter reminds us that time is the least well understood of the dimensions of space-time as currently perceived by the scientific community, even though it is fundamental to the existence of the universe. Without the passage of time there could be no motion, which is defined as the physical displacement of objects in space as time passes. Without motion there could be no planetary orbits, no manifestation of temperature dependent on molecular motion, and no circulation of blood in the bodies of animals— just to highlight a few of innumerable consequences. In short, time is the lifeblood of the universe, and without its passage, nothing would exist.

We are good at seeing objects in the three dimensional environment of space, but we can only sense time by indirectly observing its effect on things around us. Thus we have established definitions of time periods by the most familiar recurring events, such as the day and the year. We now have highly scientific ways of measuring the passage of time with enormous accuracy with atomic clocks, but these advances are merely tools to assist in the research for a fuller understanding of how time interacts with energy and matter in the universe.

The letter also points out that we are ill-equipped to comprehend concepts like infinity and entities without physical boundaries. We are predisposed to believe everything must have a beginning and an end, which are conceptually pegged as points in time. Attempting to apply such definitions to the universe could be difficult if time itself might be nonexistent at the points in question. We can only guess at such possibilities, but what is known from reliable scientific evidence is a good approximation of the age of our solar system and our planet, which is in the order of 4.5 billion years. This is a long way short of infinity, but is a length of time still hard to visualize.

The earliest fossil evidence of human existence goes back approximately two hundred thousand years. This is a tiny fraction of the geological history of Earth and would equate to just over twenty-three minutes for each year of its existence. What is remarkable about this is that humans have evolved to dominate the animal kingdom, to exercise unprecedented control of their environment, and to overpopulate the planet in such a relatively short time. It is hardly surprising that this phenomenon presages a risky future.

Geological and paleontological records of the history of life on Earth show several massive extinctions, in each of which a large percentage of prevalent species ceased to exist. The records indicate a major event approximately 450 million years ago, in which a drop in ocean temperature decimated marine life, and another 250 million years ago, when a volcanic eruption and attendant coal bed fires in Siberia is thought to have produced a fatal global winter. The evolution of the dinosaurs began after this later event, producing creatures which dominated the planet for some 150 million years until their extinction some sixty-five million years ago, believed to be caused by a massive meteorite impact. In each case, life on Earth recovered but with significant changes in dominant species. Paleontological evidence indicates that this regeneration of diversity and resurgence of population levels took many millions of years. A million years is ten thousand centuries and one hundred times longer than humans have been present on Earth in recognizable form. This is indeed a humbling perspective.

Our scientific advances have been phenomenal in the arena of understanding the interrelation of matter and energy in three-dimensional space. Albert Einstein's most famous equation, $E=mc^2$, which quantifies the equivalence of mass and energy, has been amply confirmed by experiment, and nuclear blasts have demonstrated the awesome power of such a conversion. We are competent in acceleration of objects varying in size from subatomic to space capsules achieving very high velocities in our spatial coordinates. For all that, we have not been able to change in the slightest the rate at which time passes.

In the above cited equation, c stands for the speed of light in empty space. Scientists refer to this as a universal constant, and believe it to be immutable. This one constant of physics ties together not only mass and energy but time and space through the definition of speed. Einstein's iconic theory of relativity is based upon his understanding that any proper measurement of the speed of light must give the same result in any frame of reference. We cannot answer why the speed of light is what it is—why it is not faster or slower—but we can be sure that if it were either, our universe would be vastly different. There are many other constants in Nature whose value might seem arbitrary, such as the electric charge carried by an electron. In this case too, if it were different, atomic structure would be different, the interaction of atoms with each other to make molecules would vary accordingly, and, again, our universe would be unrecognizably different. The values of Nature's physical constants are fundamental to our being, and the letter gives us at least one possible answer as to how they were set.

The Space Barrier

The stars will remain beyond our reach.

The letter tells us that human travel to destinations outside our solar system is not going to become a reality, and for similar reasons we have not been visited by aliens from interstellar space, nor are we likely to be. It is not hard to develop a practical explanation for this prediction. The technical barrier that must be overcome is dealing with the enormous distances involved and, consequently, the time that would be required for a manned interstellar journey.

The nearest star is approximately four light-years away, which means that it would take four years to get there if one could make the entire journey at the speed of light. Of course, that is not physically possible. The maximum acceleration a human being can comfortably withstand for a long time is equivalent to the force of gravity on Earth (1 g). At a constant acceleration of 1 g it would take an entire year to reach a significant fraction of the speed of light, and then it would take another year of deceleration to slow down again approaching the destination. Since the speed of light can never actually be reached by a physical body, the trip to the nearest star would take close to six years under ideal conditions. A return trip would take another six years, for a total elapsed time for the space traveler of twelve years plus the length of time spent at the destination. However, because of the relativistic speed of travel, the time elapsed on Earth during the trip would be far greater still. And this is only to the nearest star, not one with potentially habitable planets, which could be many more light-years away.

Then there is the issue of the energy required to fuel the journey. A 100 kg astronaut would require almost 5,000 watts of power to accelerate him at 1 g. For the acceleration to persist for one whole year would require an amount of energy equivalent to burning forty-five hundred liters of gasoline, weighing over 3,000 kg! Unless there is a fuel station at the other end, enough fuel must also be carried for the return trip (another 3,000 kg). Then we must add the energy required to accelerate the fuel supply to speed as well as only the payload. Quickly, it becomes apparent that the energy requirement for conventional human travel at close to light speed is enormous and nowhere near practical with today's technology. There is no foreseeable argument that could justify the cost of such an expedition on these terms.

Science fiction is not short of esoteric ideas that would make interstellar travel achievable. There are three categories of possibility. The most mundane is the low-speed traveling space colony, a massive self-contained ship in which generations would live and die during many years of flight so that their offspring could eventually arrive at a distant destination. More imaginative is the much touted hyperdrive that launches the vehicle into speeds exceeding the speed of light. This violates the known laws of physics and does not address the potentially destructive effect on the human body of the implied acceleration. Lastly there is the interstellar shortcut, or "wormhole," through which the traveler somehow tunnels into another part of the universe. This kind of phenomenon is more likely encountered in the microcosm of quantum mechanics than in the macroworld of human transportation.

Even with the most optimistic breakthroughs in the science of energy husbandry and propulsion systems, the practicality and justification for interstellar travel by humans seems impossibly remote. But what of other beings elsewhere in the galaxy? Probability is heavily in favor of the existence of intelligent civilizations in other parts of the universe, and certainly many will have reached far advanced states of knowledge and technical achievement compared to ourselves. After all, we have only been technically sophisticated for a few hundred years, whereas others may have been there thousands or even millions of years before us. Is it possible that we have been visited by emissaries of such civilizations?

Of course, aficionados of UFO phenomena claim that we have indeed been recently so visited, but probability is against this theory. Given the complexity and cost in time and energy to come here through interstellar distances, it is not logical that a visitor would not make contact or at least leave behind some identifiable evidence of having been here. Chances are that an alien visit might perhaps have taken place in the past, and if one were to occur every one hundred million years or so, the most recent one may have been in the time of the dinosaurs and evidence thereof long lost. We are not a significant solar system in the galaxy, and our galaxy is one among countless others. Our planet is overpopulated and somewhat polluted and does not seem a likely target for alien visitation. If they are smart enough to get here, they are probably too smart to stay.

The greatest motivation for interstellar travel exploited by fiction writers is the impending doom of our planet. Unavoidable collision with a large meteorite is a favorite, with historical precedents resulting in mass extinctions flavoring the story. Fortunately this type of cataclysmic event only happens rarely, with spacing of tens of millions of years. With luck, there is plenty of time for countermeasures to be developed before the next such event, and escape of any significant number of people into space is not a probable scenario. The eventual end of the world at the time of the final spasms of our sun is billions of years in the future. If humans are still occupying the planet at that time, the end will be far from sudden. It will be gradual, over generations of declining population as living conditions diminish. There is not likely to be a rush for an exit to the stars but a peaceful passing.

A Healthier Future?

Much lies ahead in the treatment of disease.

The advances in medical science have been a significant part of the technology explosion since the Industrial Revolution. Great strides have been made in treating diseases and injuries, but so much still remains to be accomplished, and there are many maladies that yet defy curative treatment, such as Parkinson's, multiple sclerosis, ALS (Lou Gehrig's), Alzheimer's, and many others, including cancer. The letter hints that our trouble in finding their successful treatment involves these diseases having roots in those dimensions that we exist in but cannot adequately perceive.

Part of the answer may lie in achieving a fuller exploitation of the human brain. Even though we have not been given the sensory organs to see in other dimensions, the brain evolved in the full spatial environment and may have the capability to access what we cannot see directly. There is already compelling evidence of this in the occasional manifestation of ESP and also in the rare incidence of savantism. Savants are people who have access to brain functions denied to most of us, resulting in phenomenal displays of memory or unusual high-level skills in music and the arts. There are well documented examples of photographic memory that demonstrate what the human brain is capable of. How this can be voluntarily achieved is not yet understood.

Apart from the possible enhancement of our learning ability through improving utilization of the brain, we have not yet begun to tap its potential to treat disease. Indeed there are many stories told of miraculous cures or remissions resulting from strong positive attitudes of the afflicted, but systematically using the power of the brain to effect medical results is still beyond our reach. A further example is the "placebo effect," which refers to a realized reduction of symptoms experienced by patients given medication with no active ingredients but with the belief that an effective medicine has been administered. In such cases the treatment has created a subconscious expectation of improvement, which the brain appears to be able to translate into reality. Many instances of using the mind to control bodily functions outside our normal experience are also documented in oriental practices involving deep meditation. These techniques are not easily assimilated and so have not yet found their way into modern medicine.

The existence of savant prodigies, displays of deep meditation, results of successful hypnotic regression, and instances of ESP and clairvoyance all give us a tantalizing hint of the possibilities to be opened to us by better understanding and using our brains. It is likely that great future advances in medicine will move beyond the prolific use of pharmaceutical drugs and more toward exploiting the self-healing capabilities within our bodies.

Big pharma—the collective name for the world's billionaire pharmaceutical corporations—has contributed hugely to the advance of medical treatment of many illnesses. However, there is a strong vested interest in the proliferation of drugs directed at alleviating the symptoms of maladies rather than treating their causes. Examples are painkillers, common cold "remedies," and antacids for relieving "heartburn." None of these big revenue producers cure the causes of the symptoms they relieve, and when they wear off, the symptoms return, and more of the medication is sought. Such noncurative medicines represent enormous profits for big pharma, and therefore represent a strong resistance lobby to deter development of natural cures that might arise from better directed brain function. In the future, medical science must move away from the predominance of chemical treatments and become more attuned to the body's capability of healing itself.

The Great Unknown

Beyond the edge.

What we do not know vastly exceeds what we do know, a state of affairs that will most certainly exist until the end of our time. The more we push forward the frontiers of science, the more we discover what we have yet to learn and the true insignificance of our humble state of knowledge of Nature. The letter refers to the analogy of the ant as an example of a being essentially living in and understanding a world of two dimensions. We have the great advantage of three-dimensional perception and have expanded our knowledge to the limits of our vision of great and small, aided by the most sophisticated tools of our technology. But we are blind in such other dimensions as most certainly exist. This blindness may be the greatest obstacle to overcome in achieving a fuller understanding of the universe.

Yet we are creatures of all dimensions, in that we and our universe itself evolved within a space comprising them all. Nature has endowed some of its creatures with sensory organs and capabilities far exceeding our own. Many have superior eyesight, others more acute hearing or sense of smell, and yet others can sense magnetic fields and some can utilize sonar guidance. Whether there are creatures that have abilities to see in other dimensions we do not yet know. The globe-spanning navigational ability of many migrating species ranging from Monarch butterflies to blue whales is still seen as miraculous, in that the mechanisms yet elude us.

Evolution continues, and there is little doubt that human beings are still in the loop of progress. What is in store for us as the generations go by? The evolutionary prerogative is adaptation to the environment and the need to survive. But the process is slow, and rapid external changes can overwhelm any hope of adaptation. Will we slowly develop even larger brains and the ability to use them more fully? Will we develop new senses of perception that will enhance our awareness of other dimensions?

These are fascinating possibilities, and only the distant future will reveal the path.

Other than the mathematical formulations beloved of theoreticians in quantum mechanics and the most modern forms of particle physics, there are other indicators of an unknown multidimensional hyperspace. The letter hints that those of us having manifested forms of ESP may in fact perceive what is hidden from the majority of us in such a hyperspace. The little understood mechanism of ESP may in fact be a rudimentary sense organ more developed in some people than in most. As with so many poorly understood manifestations, ESP is not regarded as scientific and has been commonly burdened with the trappings of occultism. The literature is full of accounts of near-death experiences, hypnotic regression into past lives, communications with the dead, and other phenomena that are difficult to substantiate or explain. Does the body of evidence suggest there is indeed access to this broader world?

The probability is good, but like the analogy given to us in the letter of trying to model a three-dimensional world by analyzing shadows on a two-dimensional screen, we face a difficult task to understand other dimensions in a useful way. One of the most promising prospects might be an enhanced ability to analyze and treat currently intractable diseases whose roots extend beyond our present ability to fathom. Whether ESP gifted people can indeed look into the future or communicate with spirits of the departed remains in the realm of speculation and is one of so many things we do not yet know.

The letter paints a grim picture for the future of the human race in its present march toward overpopulation of the planet. Clearly the ability of Earth to feed even the present masses is severely tested, as evidenced by widespread starvation in many regions. Fresh water is a dwindling resource, energy consumption is out of control, and pollution is a growing problem. Nature will inevitably solve these problems in a way yet to be seen but not likely to be pleasant.

There is, however, the promise of a future world in which a surviving human population has learned to live in harmony with its planetary environment in a sustainable way. Only then can the assimilation of knowledge and technological advances continue on the upward path initiated in the past few centuries. In such a future the true glory of the universe may be better understood and appreciated. That, after all, must be the hope and purpose of providing us with the letter.

References

Greene, B. (2004). *The Fabric of the Cosmos.* New York: Alfred A. Knopf.

Hawking, S. and Mlodinow, L. (2010). *The Grand Design.* New York: Random House Inc.

Weiss, B. L. (1988). *Many Lives, Many Masters.* New York: Simon & Schuster.